Short & Sometimes Sweet

Mary Jenkins

Short & Sometimes Sweet

Short & Sometimes Sweet
ISBN 978 1 76041 941 7
Copyright © text Mary Jenkins 2020
Cover photo by Moritz Kindler on Unsplash

First published 2020 by
Ginninderra Press
PO Box 3461 Port Adelaide 5015
www.ginninderrapress.com.au

Contents

A Simple Life	9
Peter	10
Saturday Morning Pictures	11
Shame	12
WPC 350	13
Night Duty	14
The Sex Worker	15
The Emigrant	16
After the Fire – I	17
After the Fire – II	18
Good Looking on Gumtree	19
Bungan Beach	20
No Woman is an Island	21
On Being Forty	23
On Being Eighty	24
The Trickster Brain	25
Yesday	26
Emily	27
A Blossoming of Skeletons	28
Wild Roses	29
Strangers	30
Marseille	31
It's Sunday in Paris	32
Robert Graves in Deya	33
Salvador Dali with Angels	34
Voyeurs	35
The Pea-green Mask	36
The Scarf	37
Cat	38
The Tarkine	39

Portrait of a Tree	40
Silver Peppermint	41
Land for Sale	42
Erosion	43
Pips	44
Agony & Antidotes	45
Antidotes	46
Heart Science	47
Full Moon	48
To Marry Or Not?	49
Dear One	51
Trevi Fountain	52
They Call Him Ishmael	53
Daddy Won't Be Home Tonight	54
Blue Velvet	56
The Edge of Town	58
Tidy Town	60
Nursing Home	61
Gone	62
Tidy Town Talk	63
Stars in Centrelink	64
Tidy Town's Telstra	65
The Poppies of Vercors	67
Fragments in My Head Like Shrapnel	68
A Woman in Black	69
Babylon	70
Money for Life	71
The Hammer of Witches	73
Port Arthur	74
V2 for Vengeance	76
Bumping into Jesus	77
Loaves and Fishes	78

Visiting Time	79
Nobodaddy	81
www.clonejesus.com	82
Raven's Testament	83
17 Minutes to Cygnet	85
Acknowledgements	86

Fall down seven times, stand up eight
– Japanese saying, *Presentation Zen*

A Simple Life

My mother's backlit hair
once like a horse's mane
is soft as wool pickings
in a mouse nest.

Her wrinkles deepen
around her greying eyes.
as she tries to tell me
what happened today.

She is stalled.

Down into memory
she reaches, to the time
when she knew
princesses and queens
yet chose a simple life
with the boy next door.

Silent now, she fidgets
with her tight wedding ring
remembering that boy
who died before
her youngest learnt to talk.

Peter

A baby's picture
cut from a magazine
is on the bedroom wall.
We stare at it
my sister and I.

People peep at us.
We don't know them.
Shush, they say, *shush*.

We pretend bed knobs
are fountains.
Disappointed, we look
at the picture again.

We do not understand
this is *not* our Peter.

Saturday Morning Pictures

We sit close to the front
sucking gobstoppers
ready for thrills
the Saturday treat:
Cowboys & Indians
Black Beauty or *Lassie Come Home*.

Kids shuffle shoes
rustle bags of sweets.
An organ appears
We bounce and sing along:

Mares eat oats and does eat oats
and little lambs eat ivy…

Curtains slide apart.
The picture starts with shushes
quick dips into paper bags.

A huge cock crows
when the picture ends
announcing *Pathé News*.

We're not prepared
for what comes next:
war secrets in black and white.

> Soldiers hold up people
> with their bones showing.
>
> Corpses lie in piles.

Shame

War is over.
I am five or six. Never
have I held a peach in my hand.

After hours in a queue
it's my turn.
Something happens to my heart.

I hold a peach
A golden peach with fluff
like down on a baby's crown.

I'm scared to spoil the skin.
Then I bite.

There's no juice
to trickle around my mouth
and down my chin.

There's not the tender flesh
of my dreams, only resistance
to my teeth and lips.

I cry
and am ashamed.

WPC 350

'ello, darlin', he says
take me in, will you, love

WPC 350 is in her new uniform
at the Elephant & Castle.
It's the start of her beat, solo.

Blokes nearby hear him. Grin.
Can see she's a rookie
unprepared for metho drunks.
She'll learn fast. Find the haunts
take it easy on kids that might
be better off in *in care*.

They're better at home
even if Mum's cooking's lousy.
No one's like Mum
or Dad, even though
he belts them on Fridays.

Bad day Friday.

Night Duty

A milkman's silent van
is under a crashed car.

Help me, oh God, help me

cries a man in formal suit
bloodied shirt.
Bloodied too, a woman
and her evening dress.

I clasp her head together
until an ambulance
illuminates the horror.

Gently, oh, so gently
an officer covers my hands
with the warmth of his.

He eases my fingers
from the woman's head.

The ambulance leaves:
screaming
        screaming
                screaming

The Sex Worker

Each broken nail tells a story
the young bobby could not imagine.

Joyce imagines tapered fingers
unbuttoning his blue shirt
sliding down from his chest
to feel tendrils of his fair hair.

He's a rookie, has no idea.
Joyce shows him the ropes:
the paper, the ink, the way to imprint
each unique coil of her fingertips.

This is a good night, she's sober
doesn't cuss or pull up her dress
to show her knickers are clean.

She's young but too old now
for *Care and Protection*.

This time there'll be a conviction
and a mark for life.

The Emigrant

There's no ten-pound fare
for a woman who has left
both husband and home.

All she owns is packed
in boxes covered with
cross-stitched canvas.

She huddles on deck
watches gangplanks lift
tearful emigrants embrace.

Coloured streamers snap
become headless kites.

Slowly tugged away
the *Fairsea* bellows
like a huge cow stuck in mud.

After the Fire – I

A stranger laced
sandals on my feet.
Friends brought clothes:
a toothbrush, pen and pad
put money in my pocket.
I stalled at a garage
sans cash
    sans card
        sans tout.
A man I hardly knew
paid for petrol.

There was food that night
and a bed made ready
a small girl's poem
tucked under a pillow.

Is this how the phoenix rose
when embers cooled?
Each gentle stroke
preparing her feathers for flight?

After the Fire – II

Books, more seductive
than sex or chocolates
are on my bedside table.

There's someone's love
gone wrong
a novel about naughty nuns
and there's poetry
that seeps into my dreams.

A Lonely Planet cover
mixes aqua and azure
with a shower of soft sand
that sends me flying
from debris and mud
to a South Pacific island
where I no longer think
lists of loss for the assessor
or see fire-forced pages
stuck black upon the fence.

Good looking on Gumtree

good-looking man wants…

I didn't care about good looks
and good looking he was not.
I needed help and a tenant.
He was fit, made sure of it.
No milk, no sugar, no salt
dumbbells outside the door
a large mirror – as requested.
His partner needed space.
She'd been accommodating.
His long-time wife wasn't.
The share of the split he spent
travelling, being spontaneous.
(He touches his heart).

One trial month more.
Good looks can be dreary
but he's doing a good job
painting the hall.

Bungan Beach

A butterfly rests on my hand.
Its shimmering spots
are duplicated   wing to wing:
cobalt, gold, white on black & rust
like a child's pattern on folded paper.

I sketch the scallops
of its lacy-curtain trim
as it slowly swivels searching sun.
Why here, a shadowed spot
is it sick or dying?
It flies away as I shift my arm.

This autumn day becomes tranquil.
Bees hum to a sharper trill of birds
backed by a mellow thrum of sea.
Eucalyptus leaves flicker in the breeze.
Banksia and wattle bloom yellow.
Sea salt perfumes the air.

No Woman is an Island

After the hottest day for months
and air still as held breath
lightening comes, then thunder.
Gales stop possums
thumping on the iron roof.
The full moon is overwhelmed by clouds.
Ants warned me but I ignored them.
Puddles deepen every day.
Bubbles on the puddles swell.
Some are knocked out by raindrops.
My car will not start.
I have no phone.
For days I do not talk.   Good!
There's time to read and write.
Poems shape in my head
like bubbles before they're popped.
Friends will receive letters with stamps.

I'd like some time alone I said.
Today's the fifth day, I think.

Without sun or moon or stars
days lose delineation.
My car *still* will not start.
My neighbour, a mile away
has not seen the open gate
or has not passed
or believes I wish to be alone.
Trees are agitated.
I understand them.

Fossicking for firewood
I am pelted by rain.
The car battery's flat now.
There's a long walk ahead
if my neighbour's not home.

On Being Forty

This is the time
the perfect time for love.
Nature   our genes
or dopamine
are saying *go go go*.
This is the time
for love
for procreation (last chance).
It's a time to be wild
a time for euphoria.
This is the man.
You are the woman.
This is the time
when you could die for it
die for love
knowing
that nothing   no moment
could be better
than the now
when you are together.

Like my favourite
fictional characters
I said yes to love:
yes I said *yes   yes*.

On Being Eighty

Oh how the clichés roll
off our ageing tongues:

time goes so fast.
It happens so quickly.

Things you could do yesterday
aren't as easy today.

You can imagine the stories
of doctors, of medication.

We want to get rid of things
our children don't want.

It's becoming so hard
you hear friends say.

It's becoming so hard
you hear their children say.

It's killing us.
That's a shock.

I must clean out (again).
Give more away, make lists.

I've no desire to reach ninety
expensively maintained
but I take advice
and get the handrails fitted.

The Trickster Brain

This is the time
when things go wrong
when you're old
and your brain becomes trickster.
When you wonder how it will be
if you live on and on
wise at times, fool as well.

My brain is unbalanced
or balanced   with left-handedness.
My mother named me Mary
(she believed in God then)
called me cack-handed Annie.

I became awkward
didn't learn to knit.
I pondered the left and right of vines
swirls and coils in *Midsummer Night's Dream*:

So doth the woodbine the sweet honeysuckle
Gently entwist; the female ivy so
Enrings the barky fingers of the elm…

Now I am old I need to remind
my feet to walk, my hands to grip.
Trickiest for me are numbers:
codes are lost, places too
though my words might deceive you.

Yesday

Yesterday
the bank manager said yes.
More than once he said yes
not knowing this
is my favourite word
in life and literature.

All day friends and neighbours
weeded the garden
lifted potatoes from their nests.
My coffee was extra tasty
delivered by Sam, a neighbour
with too-much-butter biscuits.

Yesterday the doctor said:
there are problems here
we can ignore them.
Just resume your healthy life.
Yes, doctor, I said
yes, I will, yes.

Emily

We're up in a golden balloon
startling animals with antlers.

Shh   shh   shhhhh.
Hot air takes Emily up.
Cold sea air pulls her down.

She's running out of gas.
We're tipping pine trees
as we go
    down
        down.

Permission to land?
A woman flees to her house.
We settle in a field.

Emily spreads her skirt
prepares for another takeoff.
Time to leave   fast.

He tips my crown:
a plastic fireman's helmet
pours champagne over my head.

Children run towards us
with posies of buttercups.

I am queen
& this is *not* a dream.

A Blossoming of Skeletons

This fossil flower
smoothed by years of caresses
no longer rests
in the hollow of her neck.

Half a life ago she sailed
in a boat with a wine-red sail
from Gotland: God's land
– though you wouldn't know it –
to a smaller isle in the Baltic Sea
where a wind-crippled juniper grew
and sheep no longer grazed.
Here was Bergman's *mise en scène*
an unlikely setting for love.

No place for a woman
who lived barefoot among
frangipani and hibiscus.
But the man at the helm
was subtle as a homing serpent
fine of touch. He sought
purity of shape in glass design.

When she looked down
– those thirty years ago –
she saw this fossil:
a blossoming of tiny skeletons
beached from ice-cold sea.
She imagined rainbows of fish
and swirling coral:
a long-gone flowering.

Wild Roses

He married me
in an ancient church
with a crystal ring
he made for me.

He married me
with a posy
of wild roses
he picked for me.

Our smiling dog
was witness
in Drev's *gamla kyrka*
where he married me.

Strangers

In the distance a dot
becomes a man.
We are alone on
on a snow-grey highway.
A road with no end
edged with pines
planted pines.
Pines with short futures.
Straight like the man
in the distance;
their tips meant for stars.

Houses are sly
hidden behind
snow-burdened trees.

Should I become lost
in this neutrality
where I am a stranger
I might not find help.

The man comes closer
on this highway without cars.
He passes.
Does not speak.
Does not look at me.
His pace –
brisk as a clerk's
on a coffee break –
does not change.

This is cold country.

Marseille

My directions
are to catch the 61 bus.

It was on strike four hours a day.
Sometimes it became number 80
changing direction.

My host forgot to mention
that to reach bus 61
I would need to take
the Metro to Vieux Port

or that it was a half-hour walk
– hot, on an August day –
from Gare St Charles
past a refugee camp
on a pitted path
that shocked the wheels
on my suitcase
past the stink of rubbish
smelling worse
than backpackers' socks.

She forgot to mention
shops would be closed.

The fridge was empty.
I expected someone younger, she said.

It's Sunday in Paris

Gendarmes roll
behind a paddy wagon
On Pont Alexandre
clearing the way
for skaters who swoop
like shearwaters
skimming along
pink-chestnut avenues.

    Gilded cherubs and nymphs
look down as young and old fly:
swarms of them, moistened
by fountains and the River Seine.

    An amber-haired girl
breaks from the flock.
Careless of traffic
she wings down a side street.

    The show is ending.
Skaters sink into seats next to us
remove bladed black boots
and swallow long drinks.

    We sip *café crème*.
Soon we will move.
There's music in the square
where fledglings practise.

A man is begging.
I give him my baguette.

What do you think I am? A fuckin' pigeon?

Robert Graves in Deya

There was a hush
in a Majorcan church
when Robert Graves arrived:
archetypal Antonio
in his Spanish hat and cape.

Hello, Robert

Delighted with his presence.
we shuffled in narrow pews
making space for two.

After every bracket
Robert clapped
before his companion
patted his arm   and they left.

Salvador Dali with Angels

I may have had a vision
after climbing many steps
and taking a side turn
en route to Sacré Coeur.

It's hot outside
cool and quiet in a chapel
where shards of gold and blue
streak from stained-glass windows.

I see Dali   devilish Dali
with his handlebar whiskers
Tucked in a corner of a window
surreal among the angels.

Voyeurs

I see him from my hotel window:
tall, hair cropped, belly rounded
beneath a gaudy shirt.

He directs traffic in the street
catches coins tossed by drivers
as he waves them into spaces.

I follow the movements of his hands.
He checks his nails
his hair, his ears, his chest.

A woman arrives
a basket slung over her shoulder.
Irritated she waits. They go.

Through my open window
I see him return   alone.

My journey is delusion.
I'm going nowhere
on this long and lonely night.

Am I a Blanche Dubois;
Mrs Stone on her *Roman Holiday*
ready to toss keys to a stranger below?

It's dark.
Curtains are drawn.
A cigarette glows
illuminating for a second
a figure hidden in shadows.

I am being watched.

The Pea-green Mask

I'm prepared in a backless gown
but not for the pea-green mask
that fastens my face to one side
flattens my nose and mouth
as I slide under a monster-machine.

With patients every twelve minutes
forty a day, I'm tiny in this universe.

Without warning I'm released.
It's like gunshots in my ear.

After fourteen visits
I can mind travel:
fruit trees bloom on the ceiling
against a shock-blue sky.
There's background musak:
cliché heaven.

I'd like Salvador Dali
to peep from a cloud;
Paul Kelly singing
'One Night the Moon'.
Then I could really travel.

The Scarf

This scarf
checked blue and green
is not a style
i would choose
but its silken softness
caresses tender
places around my neck.

After healing months
i wear it, remembering
how i found it
under a pile of beanies
in a basket of knitted gifts
left at the clinic
waiting for someone like me.

Cat

Dawn on a sun-textured track
criss-crossed with silent wallabies.
A bulldozer swings an extended claw.

Two halves of a house are coming through
on a loader needing space for an hour.
Massive trees are tossed as easily as mice.

The Tarkine

There's movement
between birds and trees and air
a quivering of the earth
on which she sits
sharing leaf futures
with minute creatures.

She looks up through branches
of ancient trees
higher than steeples
more precious than old gods
who were just as vulnerable
to politics and greed.

She will lie there
listening for eagle wingbeats
seeing every shade
of green and myrtle red
every vein of life around her
smelling deep soil as she waits.

Portrait of a Tree

Eucalyptus Globulus

Erase the fence
the sign saying DANGER.
Move the path out of the tree's way.
Colour in swift parrots   every feather.
Paint crescent leaves olive green
ochre and amber   some scarlet
veins backlit by the slipping sun.
Paint the tree as you would an old face.
Paint her at dawn   every wrinkle exposed.
Move closer to trace her veins.
Breath deeply with air from her lungs.

There's a lot of life in the old trunk yet.

Take care to detail the insects
beetles   ants   their scribbled messages.
Even for art's sake don't gild the tree
or paint it bronze like a living statue.

Let some leaves fall.
Let some bark peel to bed the young.
Caress the seeds in your pocket.

Smell a forest of eucalypts.

Silver Peppermint

Eucalyptus tenuiramis – classified *vulnerable*

Wrinkles, scars and axe-cuts
criss-cross her trunk.

From roughened bark
blood has dried amber-red.

Old skin has peeled
exposing cream and olive curves.

The hunter and his axe have gone.

There is a flourishing:
vigorous growth reaches for sky.

Blue wrens and scarlet robins
scatter twigs and seeds on our tin roof.

Land for Sale

Plots for mansions or 70 houses

The trees will go.
Space between me
and the mountain will go.

Shifting patterns of green
wind roughing rivulet water.

All will change.

Scent of eucalypts
seasoned with wattle
songs of blue-wren, raven
pied currawong and cockatoo.

All will go.

To the mountain perhaps.
The mountain will stay.
Mountains are moved

but not here   not here.

Erosion

A weathered acacia bends
to the nipple of a high slope
curved like a mother's breast
    but dry.

Tree and hill
crack and crumble.
Sheep have gone
but you can imagine
their nibble-search in grey dust
see them stiff as toys about to topple
when winds blast from the west.

Below   far below   a solitary
weatherboard cottage holds on.

There's no smoke from its chimney
to welcome a man straggling home
kindling loose in his arms.

It's four o'clock.
The time his wife
would have put the kettle on.

Pips

With hope
not expectations
I planted apple pips
and waited.

Ten years later
abundant apples grew
blushed red, white fleshed
like *Pomme de Neige*
or Ladies in the Snow.

Experienced gardeners
offered kernels of wisdom
not expecting apples to grow.

Agony & Antidotes

In an abattoir
butchers go into action.
Possums are shocked
but not quite stunned.

Five kilos of native fish
make pellets for one salmon.
Best for export.
Deformed for fertiliser.

Bushfire passes
in a national park.
Boys play football
with a smouldering possum.

Antidotes

How else will we sleep?

Paul carries a first-aid kit.
His daughter shows me teats:
one for wallabies
one for possums.

Suzie makes dog jackets
out of hemp
thylacine striped   cute
unlike her tales of extinction.

Wedge-tailed eagles circle
the smoke-stream of our fire.
Trees will grow old here
with branches strong enough for nests.

New Year's morning.
Moon bright
not quite full.
Wallaby grazing by our door.

Heart Science

Scientists report that hearts remember
pass on memories, one heart to another.

We have always known the truth
in midwives' stories, troubadours' songs.

We have known there is more
to the heart than blood and muscles.

We have felt the weight of heartache
heard our body's responding sighs.

We have known the heart's knock
tapped by a glance, the feel of a hand.

He spoke of love when she went away
touching his heart. Wanting her back.

Full Moon

He hears a woman
at an open window
howling a mensal duet
with her cat on a scratchier scale.

There's an orchestra of howls, meows
as village strays join in.
Dogs form tenor and base
noses raised to a grapefruit moon.

He plumps a pillow
around his head.
until, finally, he sleeps.

In his dream she sings
a sensuous song.
His violin harmonises
with her grey-shadowed eyes.

Her amber cat insistently
caresses his legs and purrs.

To Marry Or Not?

Darwin's question

If married
there'd be no chance
to know French
no travel to the continent
no chance to fly balloon
or take a solitary trip to Wales.

One would be forced
to visit relatives
indulge in boring gossip
miss visits to clubs
and conversations with clever men
have the anxiety of children
and the expense.

There'd be a terrible loss of time
no evening reading.

> If alone one would be free
> go where one liked
> growing wrinkly in groggy old age
> friendless, cold and childless
> working one's whole life
> like a neuter bee
> with nothing after all but words

or

with a soft wife on sofa
children (if it please God)
a friend in old age
someone to take care of the house
a warm hearth
feminine chit-chat
better for health
company that's better than a dog.

Dear One

To prepare your bed
I'll think about you.

Under a breeze-blown
sun-soaked pillowcase
I'll nestle lavender
smooth the sheets
fasten pearl buttons
on a voluptuous cover
and fluff up pillows ready
for you to read the book
I have placed close
to your bedside light.

Warmth will enfold you
like a summer wave
or the mist of a dream.

Trevi Fountain

Posed in front
of a Roman fountain
a photo shows her beauty.
Poised, he has a Clark Gable look.

Stay as sweet as you are, darling.

And she did:
her hair still long, ginger-grey
faded too her freckled skin.

Every five years they return
               toss coins
over their left shoulders
into the fountain of love.

He runs daily now
chasing his youth.

She stays at home
forever sweet.

They Call Him Ishmael

She called him my love, my dear.
Through seasons he scanned
her ocean-green eyes for a yes.

Her no clouded his heart
with a November gloom
that sent him to sea.

Rachel shivered
a shock of cold water
felt a harpoon pierce her skin
as a white whale plunged
in her dream.

With the deepest of breaths
she tightened her sails
and sped to the rescue
as Ishmael surfaced in creamy sea.

Let go the coffin keeping you safe.
Come to my arms Ishmael my love
thank God the sharks let you be.

Come home, my dearest dear.
Come to me.

Daddy Won't Be Home Tonight

Daddy's sorry to say
he's met someone else.
Yes, she is younger.
He doesn't say firmer
but his wife imagines
a pert-breasted shape
narrow at the waist
a belly that hasn't stretched
after bearing three babies.

He'll move his things on Friday.
Their flat will be ready
the furniture delivered.

He doesn't attempt to hide
the love-shine in his eyes.
She doesn't know
how to hide the panic in hers
or to live the moments
until he returns
with the not-for-her look
that shatters her heart.

She needs to sit down
but he walks to the door.

She wants to tell him
to get his things now
before the children come home
with their backpacks
of small troubles and triumphs
but after sharing sixteen years
words splinter in her mouth.

Blue Velvet

In Tidy Town
white picket fences spike
sharp-edged gardens.
Full-blown roses
follow upright tulips.
A serpentine hose
dribbles
    across
        grass.
You can see through a window
no one is watching TV
but it doesn't shut up.
Blurred figures fight.
There are gunshots
while mother quickly tidies up
clears dishes from the table
puts last night's chop bones in the bin.
She pours pink detergent in the sink
so the peanut butter jars will sparkle.

By the time Dennis parks his truck
a tray will be laid
his slippers arranged
in front of a chair
the cat is warming.
Channel 7 news will be on.

His lunchtime visit
to Mrs Brody's Blue Velvet rooms
upstairs in the local pub
will have soothed his nerves
given him an appetite for
Friday's meal of leftovers
and a stubby or five.

He can settle in
without switching channels
or wondering what Mother did today.

The Edge of Town

You can see twin peaks
snow just atom dust
on tips as thaw ends
and the river seeps
into banks, hiding
plastic, bits of fabric
a woman's stocking:
effluence and evidence.

You can hear log trucks
rolling down back roads.
A bird settles on a fir
waits for a worm.

All's well if you look
at a squad of red tulips:
upright sentinels of home
saluting white picket fences.

Even if all doesn't end well
the coffee's good and warm.
A waitress is shaped
as she should be.

In Mar T's fluorescent café
a cook is dervish dancing
twirling a hotpot
in the kitchen.
Gibberish streams
from his mouth as he twirls.

The waitress avoids him
as she swings in and out of doors
with food she would never choose to eat.

There's a cowboy waiting
wanting to know uptown fetishes
and a boyish-looking agent
who asks questions but not
what goes in the cherry pie
he likes so much.

Tidy Town

Tidy Town's Retirement Home
allows no dogs.

Pet birds are forbidden.
Children are not to play in the street.

Pegs must not be left on the line
says Grandma's Omo-bright neighbour

whose husband shat
under the house next door.

Tidy Town wins awards for trim edges
Roundup sprayed with the blackberries.

Council plans a no-rot future, with decks
and playgrounds of arsenic, zinc, and pine.

The exterminators zapped flies
in Baby John's newly painted bedroom.

Mother cleans the home with purple products
sleeps all weekend. Isn't feeling well.

Nursing Home

He's crumpled in bed
slumped sideways
    like his mouth.

A male nurse eats his food.
Stuffs the old man's mouth
with a cloth.

His daughter sees his tears
hears no words
is abused for installing a camera.

Her illegal act.

Gone

Big brooms are out in Tidy Town.

Make way for tourists.
Liners are coming into dock.

Gone is the bag lady
who played piano in the pub.

Gone the pigeon feeding
story-teller from the bus-stop.

Gone the woman fed by Christ
swathed in grey like a mummy.

Gone the woman
with a Danish pastry at her feet.

Homeless kids have disappeared
from city cavities   leaving
their marks in dark graffiti tunnels.

Tidy Town Talk

Be careful of what you say
in Tidy Town.
Words speed like Spanish flu.
Mums murmuring outside school
might shun you   and your kids.
If you say the wrong thing
you could be sued.

> On the other hand
> it's a town of kindness
> with shops where you
> get meaningful hugs.

> There are cheer up cafés
> with best barista coffee
> where you can meet someone
> to share stories   and cake.

Stars in Centrelink

A man with a clipboard controls
a slow-moving Centrelink queue.
Trim in a saucy skirt
and patterned stockings
a woman cracks a joke.
He doesn't look up.
No jokes here, I say.

We file to grumpy chairs
imagine a friendly space
not grey-dead carpet
not harsh fluoro lights
over grey plastic desks.

We imagine an intimate ambiance:
tas oak chairs and floor
desks with glowing poppies
marigolds and cornflowers.

The cheeky woman wants change:
*Liberal or Labor or Greens
as long as they're women.
That's the way to brighten things up.*

I hear my name.
Ian, neat in a blue-striped shirt
swivels his chair towards me.

If he were not in this toxic place
he'd be out with his telescope.
We talk of stars.
The way tourists marvel at our skies.

Tidy Town's Telstra

Telstra signs
are everywhere:
huge over a Tech Bar
lined with bar-stools.
A perfect height for me.

Experts move in
laptops in hand.
This is their space.

Suited men stride
faux-wood floors.
Clip, clip, clip
go their shoe studs.
as if in high heels.

A dance could be coming on.

Toxic Telstra's pretend bedroom
has pretend books
pretend family photos
an empty pink piggybank.

You could lie on a beanbag
listen to a million tunes.

I perch on a grey square pouf
next to other squares:
bright pink, lime green, blue.
We're bookended by a couple
who complain across me.

Woman with red scarf
is written on a clipboard.
My turn has come.

Kathryn with a Y
not an I takes over.
She asks how I am.
Doesn't look at me.
Is worried.
Her exams are tomorrow.
She gets headaches.

After a tiresome questionnaire
essential for connections
she puts a large-letter telephone
into a Telstra plastic bag
and   almost   smiles.

The Poppies of Vercors

Black centres of poppies
are reminders of Resistance:
deaths in the mountains.

Long silences in the villages.

Who betrayed men and women
in mountain hideouts?

Years later old women
tell stories
as they remember them
but not all they know.

Best to forgive but not to forget.

Poppies patch the roadside
black, flared with unforgettable red.

Fragments in My Head Like Shrapnel

A poet engineer from Babylon
came to Australia between wars.

Friends left behind had been silent for a month.

The poet regrets he has only fifteen minutes.
No time to speak of ancient civilisations:
poems, epics, stories linking all of us
and his imprisonment for a poem
with indictable words: *Black March*.

The poet finds it hard to speak.
He cries as he tells us this story:

In the aftermath of the first Gulf War
thousands of his people died.
Unprotected by *Liberating Forces*
He and his family fled to a village.
He stopped when he saw a woman
kneeling at the roadside
weeping over a young girl's body
and singing.

The woman tells him she is singing
to stop a hovering bird
from taking part of her child
or any sign that might show who killed her.

A Woman in Black

She imagines a woman her own age
crouched low in the dusk.

This distant but close woman waits
for a pan of water to boil on a fire
carefully built with grass and small sticks.
She dips dry biscuits in grey tea-water
made from grass and wild herbs.
Her back teeth are missing
the front ones sparse.
Two chipped bowls are on a bench
but there is no stew.
Warehouses have been emptied
before expected strikes.
She draws a shawl over her head
and waits. She waits for bombs.

Her granddaughter sleeps
in a taped-up room.

Babylon

Gilgamesh said,
Go unto the wall of Uruk
examine its foundations
inspect the brickwork thoroughly…

Thousands of soldiers
march through Ishtar's Gate.

Every day they stamp
past the Lion of Babylon.

Tanks crush the cuneiform boasts
of King Nebuchadnezzar.

Stories of antiquity in mud bricks
are removed in sandbags.

Toxic gravel forms foundations
of helipads, car parks and barracks.

The Minister for Culture
graciously thanks *friendly forces*
for the handover of the site.

Money for Life

They're counting the billions
Bush's war could cost.
Like you'd budget a holiday
they say:

shall we go now
or shall we wait for weather
that's cooler for troops?

What date do you think is best?

Should we go now
before marches are held
and politicians' popularity dips?
Shall we send in the bombs?

If there's a veto on war
shall we bring back the troops
before they've had a good round?

> But what of the people
> who'll die with the soldiers:
> the children, their mothers
> the old and the sick?

> What of those suffering
> from sanctions and scarcities
> with no one to help them.
> Where could they flee
> when nobody wants them?
> What will we do if they
> arrive in old boats to our shores?

And the cost?
What would it take
to repair this poor country?

Will there be birds left to sing?

Will there be spring?

The Hammer of Witches

Malleus Maleficarum (1487)

i would not escape
these men in black

bible in one hand
Malleus in the other

they'd find bruises on my arm
see herbs in my garden

display my wicker broom
and my black cat in court

they'd swear i make penises
go up or down

>   if my head
>   stayed above water
>   the cardinals would all agree
>   i should die   i should die
>   burned at the stake

Port Arthur

1 May 1996

This slowly healing site
of green-turfed pasture
and supported stones
translates an ugly past
into soothing entertainment.

Port Arthur cracks open
in a series of gun blasts
from a young man
who seems to have everything.

Tasmania's demented days
and a friend's decision
not to live pitch into me.

On this, the third day
I raise my head
to look evil in the eye
of a television set.

I cry with the nurse
who couldn't put everything
together again.

On the radio a woman
mourns thirty-five deaths
and those still uncounted
for whom the bells toll.

Charged with murder
the man has treatment for his burns.
His mother suffers in requested solitude.

V2 for Vengeance

I see a bird
through my skylight.
It swirls   dives
becomes a rocket.

There are wails:
oh, those undulating wails.
The relief of an *All Clear*.

Sheltered under stairs
we wait.

Our mother returns
her face shock-white
rubble-dust covers her coat.

Eighteen in one family
and kids we knew
dead.
All dead.

Killed by a V2 rocket.

Bumping into Jesus

When he said *hello, Mary*
I was amazed.
Didn't expect to see Him in Hobart
going to the fish punts at the docks.

He touched me as he passed
his hand soft as a schoolgirl's.

Perhaps he gets fish here every night.
Yes, I'll be here, Jesus.
I'll help you with the loaves & fishes
share things out.
There's nothing I wouldn't do for you.
Fancy you remembering me.

The water's not good
don't you walk on it
those foreign starfish
mess things up.
There's oil & wrappings
in the river from fish & chips.
Don't eat the fried stuff
I'll tell him.
The oil isn't what it used to be
from those silver olive trees.

It must feel odd
turning up in a place like this.
I really must take care of him.

He knows me.

Loaves and Fishes

Fish are belly-up on the beach
and the loaves?
Baking's getting beyond me:
too many people, drought
grain used for fuel
polluted flour.
It could make you mad.
Never did I imagine this could happen.

The faithful share when they can
bless them
but now they're stargazing
beginning to doubt.
Imagine if *I* poisoned our people
they're not looking well as it is.
The disciples are getting old.
Peter's grumpier than ever.
Mary?
She helps with the baking
brings her friends.
We get very little sleep
stop when flour runs out
and we hope, oh Lord we hope
there'll be grain tomorrow
to feed the thousands in the queues.

Visiting Time

When I first met Jesus
I thought he was quite ordinary.
Men I like are solid
the sort you can lean on.
He's not like that.
He's puny really.
But there's something about him.
When he looks at me, listening
– he's good at that –
I feel he's drawing me into him.
Can't resist him.
I stroke him:
his hair, his arms, his hands
even his nails
so clean and baby pink.
Not like mine.
His eyes are blue
not just blue
they're fringed with green
black-centred like a wildflower
with sun-touched lashes, baby-fine.
He smells nice, woody
like the pine cones I put on my fire.

Jack's not in the picture.
Well, only sometime
when I'm feeling weary
after the cleaning.
He used to rub my back in the bath
hard, I liked that.

No one rubs my back now.
There was a nurse who did
but they shouted at her.
She's gone.
Jesus doesn't leave me.
When it's dark
and other people have left
when I feel awful
and the pills don't help.
He stays here.
Jesus wouldn't hurt my baby.
Red wobble, yellow wobble
jelly on the plate.
We'll share it.
Not his favourite dish though
but Jesus never complains
not after what he's been through.
I listen to his stories
and the ones the night nurse tells.
She said he tries to do such a lot
making food go round
fixing up people rotten with disease.
He even walked on water.
I flooded the bathroom when I tried.
Sister was ratty about that.
He couldn't even trust his friends
but he can trust me. I believe in him.

Draw the curtains and go. Go.
We want to be alone now.

Nobodaddy

(Fool for love: Sam Shepard)

No wonder he lurks in the shadows
this old man god sucking his pipe
in front of a collapsing shed
his hat shading wretched eyes.

Is he thinking of his faulty Creation
his incestuous progeny
the droughts the wars
murders that began with the brothers?

Perhaps I should feel sorry for him.
His loneliness when we deserted
but with the indifference
he has shown it's difficult to care.

www.clonejesus.com

Jeez! 'Ave a look 'ere.

There's these two blokes in Berkeley California
wot finks the Secon' Comin's takin' too long
bin waitin' two fousand years they sed
they're gonna make it 'appen.

Bitta DNA from the tourin shroud
or some uver Jesus relic
then all they'll need's a virgin.
Yer can check it out on the web
that's if yer've got one.

An' 'ere, ova from the sportin' page
Chickens Turned Into Drug Labs
bitta DNA in their eggs.

Whatsit matta
eggs is eggs
chickens in us
us in chickens
we gotta be saved, eh?

This'll give 'em somefin' to talk about on Sundy.
Tear it out fer the missus, will yer?
Check the uva side but
done wanna miss nofin' important.

DNA   dinna orta 'appen'
'e comes back every bloomin' Christmas any 'ow.
Whatyer fink, mate?

Raven's Testament

Enough of the dove
carrying an olive branch
the pure dove
the Christian dove
the insidious coo-cooing dove.

Six days and seven nights
we were stuck at Mount Nimush.
It was disgusting in the Ark
with those smelly animals.

The dove flew out first.
She came back.
No branch in her beak.

I touched land after the Deluge.
With my golden vision
I spotted the olive tree
waving silver-tipped leaves
sun-sheen on my brilliant
black wings as I soared.

It was me   mee   mee!
I saw the ebbing of waters.

It's there in the Epic
written on tablets
long before Picasso
painted his *Dove with Olive Branch*.

Imagine if his bird had been black.
I wouldn't be forgotten then.

Black is beautiful.
All that whiteness, cleanliness and purity.
Argh
      Argh
           Aaaaargh.

17 Minutes to Cygnet

Wattles along the river
are startling in bloom
spring still weeks away.

Swans on marshland
are massed: silent, black.
The river, sinuous and still
reflects companion trees.

It's bliss to quit the highway
past sheep crowded on a block
past bulbous men, one finger raised
in salute. Their little dogs on leads.

A right turn at the post office.
Up to where the road greets hills
           and I'm home.

Acknowledgements

Ralph Wessman gave me a start as a published writer in his literary journal *The Famous Reporter* in March 2006. He continued his support until his retirement. My heartfelt thanks to him. Pete Hay, my PhD supervisor, sent me in Ralph's direction and will always have my thanks for his support and friendship. My writing companions Gina Mercer, Lyn Reeves and Anne Collins generously proofread and critiqued my work and insisted I complete this collection. Without them it would not exist. Justy Phillips and Margaret Woodward encouraged me to 'leave a trace' by including me with 112 writers in the Salamanca Arts Project: *The People's Library 2018. A Published Event.* Their collaboration of art and writing came with a message of encouragement: 'Don't stop here.'

Mary Jenkins

www.ingramcontent.com/pod-product-compliance
Lightning Source LLC
Chambersburg PA
CBHW070049120526
44589CB00034B/1676